United States Government Accountability Office

Report to Congressional Requesters

I0448823

November 2013

CLIMATE CHANGE

Federal Efforts Under Way to Assess Water Infrastructure Vulnerabilities and Address Adaptation Challenges

GAO-14-23

November 2013

CLIMATE CHANGE

Federal Efforts Under Way to Assess Water Infrastructure Vulnerabilities and Address Adaptation Challenges

GAO Highlights

Highlights of GAO-14-23, a report to congressional requesters

Why GAO Did This Study

The effects of climate change on water resources have already been observed and are expected to continue. The Corps and Reclamation own and operate key water resource management infrastructure, such as dams and reservoirs. Adaptation—adjustments in natural or human systems to a new or changing environment that exploits beneficial opportunities or moderates negative effects—can be used to help manage the risks to vulnerable resources. In 2009, a law—commonly referred to as the SECURE Water Act—and a presidential executive order directed federal agencies to address the potential impacts of climate change.

GAO was asked to review agency actions to address climate change impacts on water infrastructure. This report examines (1) actions taken by the Corps and Reclamation since 2009 to assess and respond to the potential effects of climate change on water infrastructure and (2) challenges, if any, faced by the Corps and Reclamation in assessing and responding to the potential effects of climate change on water infrastructure, and the steps the agencies are taking to address them. GAO analyzed the agencies' climate change adaptation guidance and planning documents and interviewed agency officials and other key stakeholders, including water users, environmental groups, and researchers.

GAO is not making any recommendations.

View GAO-14-23. For more information, contact Steve Morris at (202) 512-3841 or morriss@gao.gov.

What GAO Found

The Department of Defense's U.S. Army Corps of Engineers (Corps) and the Department of the Interior's Bureau of Reclamation (Reclamation) have assessed water resource and infrastructure vulnerabilities and taken steps to develop guidance and strategies to adapt to the effects of climate change. Specifically, since 2009, the Corps has completed a high-level assessment of the vulnerabilities to climate change of various agency missions. The assessment found, for example, that the effects of increasing air temperatures on glaciers could negatively impact mission areas including navigation and flood damage reduction. The Corps has also conducted pilot studies to help identify adaptation guidance and strategies; it has completed 5 of the 15 pilot studies initiated and plans to start another study in 2013. Similarly, Reclamation has completed baseline assessments of the potential impacts of climate change on future water supplies for the major river basins where it owns and operates water management infrastructure. Reclamation, in collaboration with nonfederal entities, is now conducting more focused assessments, known as Basin Studies, through which Reclamation seeks to identify water supply vulnerabilities and project future climate change impacts on the performance of water infrastructure. According to agency officials, these studies will also help Reclamation develop adaptation strategies to address these impacts, such as operational or physical changes to existing water infrastructure or development of new facilities. Three Basin Studies have been completed, an additional 14 are under way, and 2 more are planned. Reclamation next plans to initiate feasibility studies for adaptation strategies identified in completed Basin Studies. Both agencies are incorporating what they have learned from their efforts into agency policies, planning, and guidance, according to agency officials.

In 2009, the Corps, Reclamation, the National Oceanic and Atmospheric Administration, and the U.S. Geological Survey (USGS), jointly published a study that identified several challenges that climate change poses for water resource managers, and the Corp and Reclamation are collaboratively addressing these challenges. Specifically, these agencies are

- identifying the data and tools needed by water managers to address climate change, which will help guide federal research efforts;
- obtaining needed climate data by collaborating with other agencies to help ensure that the data are collected, such as by sharing some costs associated with maintaining USGS's stream flow measurement activities, which are valuable to Corps water planning and management;
- integrating climate science into water resource management decision making through activities such as developing and communicating science to inform climate adaptation strategies; and
- collaborating in the development of a climate change science training program for federal and nonfederal water resources managers.

The Corps and Reclamation have collaborated together and with others in a manner that is generally consistent with practices that GAO has identified as important to enhancing and sustaining collaboration among agencies. The Corps and Reclamation have made collaboration a key element of their policy and plans for adapting to the effects of climate change and have reinforced accountability for collaboration through agency performance management systems.

_____ United States Government Accountability Office

Contents

Abbreviations

CCAWWG	Climate Change and Water Working Group
Corps	U.S. Army Corps of Engineers
Interior	U.S. Department of the Interior
NOAA	National Oceanic and Atmospheric Administration
Reclamation	Bureau of Reclamation
Task Force	Interagency Climate Change Adaptation Task Force
USGS	U.S. Geological Survey
WWCRA	West-Wide Climate Risk Assessment

GAO

U.S. GOVERNMENT ACCOUNTABILITY OFFICE

441 G St. N.W.
Washington, DC 20548

November 14, 2013

The Honorable Barbara Boxer
Chairman
Committee on Environment and Public Works
United States Senate

The Honorable Max Baucus
United States Senate

The Honorable Dick Durbin
United States Senate

The Honorable Harry Reid
United States Senate

The Honorable Mark Udall
United States Senate

The Honorable Tom Udall
United States Senate

According to recent scientific studies, including those conducted by the U.S. Global Change Research Program,[1] climate-related changes—including increases in air and water temperatures, changes in precipitation patterns, reduced snow cover, retreating glaciers, and rising sea levels—will likely adversely affect many aspects of the natural environment in the United States.[2] The U.S. Department of the Interior's (Interior) U.S. Geological Survey (USGS) has reported that of all the potential threats posed by climate change, those associated with water

---

[1]The U.S. Global Change Research Program coordinates and integrates federal research on changes in the global environment and their implications for society. Led by a team of officials from each of the U.S. Global Change Research Program's 13 participating departments and agencies, the U.S. Global Change Research Program engages in a variety of activities designed to strengthen and strategically direct climate change research in the United States and improve the flow of that information to federal, state, and local decision makers, and the public.

[2]Thomas R. Karl, Jerry M. Melillo, and Thomas C. Peterson, eds., U.S. Global Change Research Program, *Global Climate Change Impacts in the United States* (New York, New York: Cambridge University Press, 2009).

GAO-14-23 Climate Change Adaptation

resources are arguably the most consequential for both society and the environment.[3] The effects of climate change on water resources have already been observed and are expected to continue. For example, a shift in the form of precipitation from snow to rain and earlier melting of mountain snowpack has been documented in western states. This change in precipitation is expected to result in a decrease in the amount of reliable water supply in areas where snow has been a major source. As we reported in October 2009,[4] policymakers are increasingly viewing adaptation—defined by the National Research Council as adjustments in natural or human systems to a new or changing environment that exploits beneficial opportunities or moderates negative effects—as a risk-management strategy to protect vulnerable resources that might be affected by changes in the climate.[5] GAO added limiting the federal government's fiscal exposure by better managing climate change risks to our 2013 update of high-risk areas because of the government's role, among other things, as the owner or operator of extensive infrastructure.[6]

The Department of Defense's U.S. Army Corps of Engineers (Corps) and Interior's Bureau of Reclamation (Reclamation) own and operate key water resource management infrastructure, such as canals, dams, and reservoirs, that may be affected by climate change. The Corps is the largest and oldest federal water management agency, with water resources and infrastructure in every state authorized for specific purposes such as navigation, flood and coastal storm damage reduction, hydropower, and water supply, among other things. Established in 1902, Reclamation constructed dams, reservoirs, power plants, and canals in 17 western states, and today is the second largest producer of hydroelectric power in the western United States and the largest wholesaler of water in the nation. The Corps and Reclamation work with each other and with other federal agencies, such as the Department of Commerce's National Oceanic and Atmospheric Administration (NOAA)

---

[3]Lins, Harry F., Hirsch, Robert M., and Kiang, Julie, *Water—the Nation's Fundamental Climate Issue: A White Paper on the U.S. Geological Survey Role and Capabilities: U.S. Geological Survey Circular 1347 (2010).*

[4]GAO, *Climate Change Adaptation: Strategic Federal Planning Could Help Government Officials Make More Informed Decisions,* GAO-10-113 (Washington, D.C.: Oct. 7, 2009).

[5]National Research Council, *America's Climate Choices: Adapting to the Impacts of Climate Change* (Washington, D.C.: 2010).

[6]GAO, *High-Risk Series: An Update,* GAO-13-283 (Washington, D.C.: February 2013).

and USGS, which collect and interpret weather and climate information that is valuable for effective water resource management. In addition, the Corps and Reclamation coordinate with state and local water resource managers and other stakeholders who are responsible for water resources activities within their jurisdictions to manage water for agricultural, municipal, and conservation uses, among others.

Congress and the Executive Office of the President have directed federal agencies to address the potential impacts of climate change. In 2009, a law—commonly referred to as the SECURE Water Act—was enacted, requiring, among other things, that Reclamation establish a climate change adaptation program to (1) assess the effect of and risk resulting from global climate change on the quantity of water resources and (2) develop strategies to address potential water shortages and other impacts.[7] Reclamation was also required to report to relevant congressional committees its progress implementing the act within 2 years of passage and every 5 years thereafter. Also in 2009, the President signed Executive Order 13514,[8] calling for federal agencies to participate in the existing Interagency Climate Change Adaptation Task Force (Task Force). The executive order directed the Task Force to develop federal recommendations for adapting to climate change impacts both domestically and internationally and to recommend key components to include in a national strategy. Based on the Task Force recommendations, the President's Council on Environmental Quality issued implementing instructions directing federal agencies to, among other things, establish an agency climate change adaptation policy and deliver to the council and the Office of Management and Budget a climate adaptation plan for implementation in fiscal year 2013.[9]

You requested that we review the climate adaptation efforts of the Corps and Reclamation. This report examines (1) the actions the Corps and Reclamation have taken since 2009 to assess and respond to the potential effects of climate change on water infrastructure and (2) what

---

[7]Pub. L. No. 111-11, tit. IX, subtit. F (2009).

[8]Executive Order 13514, *Federal Leadership in Environmental, Energy, and Economic Performance*, October 5, 2009. 74 Fed. Reg. 52117 (Oct. 5, 2009).

[9]*Instructions for Implementing Climate Change Adaptation Planning in Accordance with Executive Order 13514, Federal Leadership in Environmental, Energy, and Economic Performance*, March 4, 2011.

challenges, if any, the Corps and Reclamation face in assessing and responding to the potential effects of climate change on water infrastructure, and the steps the agencies are taking to address them.

To describe what actions the Corps and Reclamation have taken to assess and respond to the potential effects of climate change since 2009, we reviewed and analyzed federal law, an executive order, and relevant guidance to identify the climate change impact assessment and adaptation activities that the Corps and Reclamation are directed to perform. We reviewed and analyzed the agencies' orders, policy, and program guidance and interviewed agency officials to determine how the Corps and Reclamation have interpreted and implemented federal laws and orders. We also reviewed and analyzed documentation, such as reports, studies, and plans, and interviewed agency officials, as well as other water resource managers and climate science specialists to gather information on what the Corps and Reclamation have done to assess and respond to the potential effects of climate change on existing and planned federal water infrastructure investments. We identified and selected the resource managers and climate science specialists using an iterative process, soliciting names from agency officials and others we interviewed, and selecting those identified as having a high level of participation and knowledge. From among those identified, we conducted semistructured interviews to obtain their views on the Corps' and Reclamation's efforts to assess and respond to the potential effects of climate change. We did not assess the Corps' and Reclamation's actions to implement specific climate change adaptation planning frameworks or steps because their efforts are in the early stages. We used in-house scientific expertise to analyze the soundness of the methodological approaches utilized in selected documents, and we determined them to be sufficiently sound for our purposes. Relevant assessments, reports, and studies are cited throughout this document.

To describe what challenges, if any, the Corps and Reclamation face in assessing and responding to the potential effects of climate change on water infrastructure, as well as steps these agencies are taking to address these challenges, we reviewed and analyzed agency documents, including planning documents and assessments of efforts to date. We also reviewed and analyzed documentation of actions taken by the Corps, Reclamation, and other water managers to help mitigate these challenges, and we assessed the extent to which these efforts have been collaborative based on prior GAO work.[10] In addition, we spoke with agency officials, as well as sought the perspectives of state and local water managers and climate specialists, to learn about the challenges faced by the Corps and Reclamation and the steps the agencies have taken to address them. We selected these managers and specialists using an iterative process, based on recommendations of agency officials and others we interviewed. From among those identified, we conducted semistructured interviews about challenges and potential steps to address them and conducted a content analysis of their responses.

We conducted this performance audit from October 2012 to November 2013 in accordance with generally accepted government auditing standards. Those standards require that we plan and perform the audit to obtain sufficient, appropriate evidence to provide a reasonable basis for our findings and conclusions based on our audit objectives. We believe that the evidence obtained provides a reasonable basis for our findings and conclusions based on our audit objectives.

Background

Climate change is having a variety of impacts on natural resources in the United States, ranging from more severe drought to increased flooding, and is altering assumptions that have been central to water resource planning and management. Congress and the Executive Office of the President have directed federal agencies to address the potential impacts of climate change. The two key federal water resource management agencies included in this review—the Corps and Reclamation—have similar yet distinct roles in managing water for a wide variety of purposes. In addition to the water management challenges posed by climate change, both agencies are dealing with aging water management infrastructure with limited funding for maintenance and construction.

---

[10]GAO, *Results-Oriented Government: Practices That Can Help Enhance and Sustain Collaboration among Federal Agencies*, GAO-06-15 (Washington, D.C.: Oct. 21, 2005).

Potential Climate Change Impacts on Water Resources Can Be Addressed through Adaptation Planning

According to the U.S. Global Change Research Program, changes in the climate in the United States and its coastal waters have altered—and will continue to alter—the water cycle, affecting where, when, and how much water is available for all uses. Changes in the climate—including warmer temperatures, changes in precipitation patterns, rising sea levels, and more frequent and intense storms—affect water resources in a number of ways such as increased flooding in some areas and drought in others, and inundation and erosion in coastal areas. Precisely how and to what extent changes in the climate will affect particular water resources in the future is uncertain, but climate-related changes are expected to continue and increase in intensity in some areas of the nation.

Climate change has the potential to affect many aspects of the environment and society in which water resource management plays an active role. A 2011 federal interagency review of the potential impacts of climate change on water resources identified four interrelated areas of concern for water resource managers as follows[11]:

- assuring an adequate water supply for multiple needs, such as drinking water, agriculture, energy production, industrial uses, navigation, and recreation;
- protecting life, health, and property in the face of risks posed by climate change;
- protecting the quality of freshwater resources, including the quality of surface water and groundwater, and the health of fisheries and aquatic habitat; and
- protecting coastal and ocean resources as rising sea levels and changes in storm frequency, intensity, and duration impact coastal infrastructure.

Adaptation—defined by the National Research Council as adjustments in natural or human systems to a new or changing environment that exploits beneficial opportunities or moderates negative effects—is an element of the proposed responses to climate change that is gaining more attention. More specifically, policymakers are increasingly viewing adaptation as a risk-management strategy to protect vulnerable sectors and communities that might be affected. As we reported in our May 2013 report on land

---

[11]Federal Interagency Panel on Climate Change and Water Data and Information, 2011, *Report to Congress—Strengthening the scientific understanding of climate change impacts on freshwater resources of the United States*, 49.

resource management agency adaptation efforts, climate change adaptation planning frameworks generally consist of four key elements that are reviewed and revised as needed as new information emerges.[12] These four elements are the following:

- Establish a mandate to address climate change with clearly articulated adaptation goals, objectives, and measures of success toward meeting goals.
- Assess and understand the risks, vulnerabilities, and opportunities posed by climate change by determining (1) what aspects of the climate are changing and over what periods, (2) which resources will be most at risk, (3) why these resources are likely to be vulnerable, and (4) what uncertainties are associated with the predicted climate change impacts and how this may impact adaptation efforts.
- Develop and prioritize management adaptation actions; that is, determine how to respond to the identified risks by considering a wide array of possible adaptation measures and identifying the highest priority adaptation measures.
- Implement management options, evaluate the results to determine the actions' effectiveness, and makes adjustments as necessary. As climate continues to change, adaptation actions need to be regularly monitored for effectiveness and plans need to incorporate new information about risks, lessons learned, and modified priorities.

According to a 2009 study collaboratively produced by the Corps, NOAA, Reclamation, and USGS,[13] a variety of water-management options might be considered to facilitate adaptation to climate change, including operational changes, demand management, and infrastructure changes. The study concluded that the options for responding to the effects of climate change will vary by location, and that evaluating options will likely require a partnership between federal, state, and local interests to attain consensus among water managers and users.

---

[12]GAO, *Climate Change Various Efforts Are Under Way at Key Natural Resources Management Agencies,* GAO-13-253 (Washington, D.C.: May 31, 2013).

[13]L.D. Brekke, J.E. Kiang, J.R. Olsen, R.S. Pulwarty, D.A. Raff, D.P. Turnipseed, R.S. Webb, and K.D. White, *Climate change and water resources management—A federal perspective: USGS Circular 1331 (2009).*

Federal Agencies Have Been Directed to Address Climate Change Adaptation

In 2009, Congress passed the SECURE Water Act, requiring Reclamation to establish a climate change adaptation program to (1) assess the effect of and risk resulting from global climate change on the quantity of water resources and (2) develop strategies to address potential water shortages and other impacts.[14] To assess the effect of climate change, the law requires Reclamation to analyze the extent to which changes in water supply will impact several areas, including Reclamation's ability to deliver water to its customers, hydroelectric power generation, fish and wildlife habitat, and recreation. The law requires Reclamation to assess specific risks to the water supply of each of its major river basins, including risks related to, among other things, changes in snow cover and the timing and quantity of runoff. To develop strategies to address impacts, the law requires Reclamation, in consultation with nonfederal stakeholders such as appropriate state water resource agencies, to consider and develop appropriate strategies to mitigate the impacts of water supply changes, such as strategies for modifying reservoir storage or operating guidelines and water conservation.[15]

Also in 2009, the President signed Executive Order 13514, Federal Leadership in Environmental, Energy, and Economic Performance which, among other things, directs agencies to participate in the Interagency Climate Change Adaptation Task Force (Task Force), which was already developing a strategy for adaptation to climate change, and to develop approaches through which the policies and practices of the agencies can

---

[14]Pub. L. No. 111-11, tit. IX, subtit. F (2009).

[15]In addition, the law requires Reclamation to (1) coordinate with USGS, NOAA, and appropriate state water resource agencies to ensure that its climate change program has access to the best available scientific information on presently observed and projected future impacts of global climate change on water resources; (2) consult with other federal and applicable state agencies to develop a monitoring plan to acquire and maintain water resources information; and (3) submit a report to relevant congressional committees that describes, among other things, the results of its assessments and analysis, the mitigation strategies developed and implementation of the monitoring plans within 2 years of its passage, and every 5 years thereafter.

be made compatible with the Task Force's strategy.[16] In October 2010, the Task Force delivered a progress report to the President through the Council on Environmental Quality containing overarching policy goals to advance climate adaptation and recommending the development of a national action plan to strengthen climate change adaptation for freshwater resources.[17] Based on the work of the Task Force, the Council on Environmental Quality subsequently issued detailed adaptation planning implementation instructions in March 2011.[18] The instructions directed the agencies to issue an agency-wide climate change adaptation policy statement, complete a high-level analysis of agency vulnerability to climate change, and submit to the Council on Environmental Quality and the Office of Management and Budget their climate adaptation plans by June 4, 2012, for implementation in fiscal year 2013.[19]

The Corps and Reclamation Construct, Operate, and Manage Federal Water Infrastructure

For over 230 years, the Corps has led the development and stewardship of much of the nation's public water resources. The Corps' Civil Works Program plans and manages water for transportation, recreation, energy, wildlife habitat, aquatic ecosystems, and water supply, while reducing the impacts of flood damages and other natural disasters. Specifically, the Corps has constructed—and continues to operate, maintain, and rehabilitate—a large inventory and wide variety of water management

---

[16]In our 2013 High-Risk Update, we noted that while individual agency actions are necessary, a centralized strategy driven by a government-wide plan is also needed to reduce the federal fiscal exposure to climate change, maximize investments, achieve efficiencies, and better position the government for success. Even then, such approaches will not be fully sufficient unless also coordinated with decisions at the state and local levels that drive much of the federal government's fiscal exposure. The challenge is to develop a cohesive approach at the federal level that also informs action at the state and local levels.

[17]Council on Environmental Quality, *Progress Report of the Interagency Climate Change Adaptation Task Force: Recommended Actions in Support of a National Climate Change Adaptation Strategy*, October 5, 2010.

[18]Council on Environmental Quality, *Federal Agency Climate Change Adaptation Planning, Implementing Instructions* and *Federal Agency Climate Change Adaptation Planning, Support Document,* March 4, 2011.

[19]In addition, as recommended in the 2010 progress report, the Task Force issued the *National Action Plan—Priorities for Managing Freshwater Resources in a Changing Climate* in October 2011, which established a goal for managing water resources in a changing climate, identified key recommendations to achieve that goal, and described specific supporting actions that federal agencies should take to implement the recommendations.

infrastructure, including reservoirs, hydropower facilities, commercial inland waterways, harbors, and levee systems. In June 2011, in response to the implementing instructions for Executive Order 13514, the Corps established its adaptation policy statement for addressing the effects of climate change, which called for the integration of climate change adaptation in all Corps activities.[20] Two Corps programmatic efforts—the Interagency Performance Evaluation Task Force/Hurricane Protection Decision Chronology Lessons Learned Implementation Team (also known as Actions for Change) and the Responses to Climate Change Program—support the Corps' ongoing adaptation activities.

Since 1902, Reclamation has carried out its mission to manage, develop, and protect water and related resources in 17 western states. The agency has led or provided assistance in constructing most of the large dams and water diversion structures in the West for the purpose of developing water supplies for irrigation—that is, "reclaiming" these lands for human use. In 2009, Reclamation directed its Office of Research and Development and its Office of Policy and Administration to take the lead in implementing the actions required by the SECURE Water Act. Reclamation's climate adaptation efforts fall within the larger effort by Interior to, among other things, implement Executive Order 13514. In 2013, Interior adopted a policy directing the agency to integrate climate change adaptation strategies into its operations, policies, programs, and planning. See appendix I for more information on the Corps' and Reclamation's organization and infrastructure.

In addition to each agency's individual efforts, the Corps and Reclamation established a partnership in 2007—the Climate Change and Water Working Group (CCAWWG)—to address their mutual concerns about the potential effects of climate change on their agencies' missions.[21] In 2009,

---

[20]The USACE Climate Change Adaptation Policy Statement issued June 3, 2011, established a Climate Change Adaptation Steering Committee to oversee and coordinate agency-wide climate change adaptation planning and implementation. The Corps' Climate Change Adaptation Steering Committee is chaired by the Chief, Engineering and Construction. The Assistant Secretary of the Army for Civil Works was designated as the USACE Senior Adaptation Point of Contact responsible for ensuring implementation of the Corps' adaptation policy.

[21]In addition to the Corps and Reclamation, founding CCAWWG members included USGS and NOAA—two key climate science agencies. CCAWWG has since expanded to include, among others, the U.S. Environmental Protection Agency, Federal Emergency Management Agency, National Aeronautics and Space Administration, and U.S. Department of Agriculture.

GAO-14-23 Climate Change Adaptation

the CCAWWG partners jointly produced a preliminary assessment of how climate could impact federal water resources management, which explored strategies to improve water management by tracking, anticipating, and responding to climate change, and identified adaptation challenges.[22]

Agencies Manage Climate Change Risk While Facing Aging Infrastructure

According to a 2012 National Research Council report on Corps infrastructure,[23] large portions of the Corps' water resources infrastructure were built over 50 years ago and are experiencing various stages of decay and disrepair, making project maintenance and rehabilitation a high priority. The report also found that federal funding over the past 20 years has consistently been inadequate to maintain the Corps' infrastructure at acceptable levels of performance and efficiency. Similarly, most of Reclamation's water infrastructure facilities are more than 50 years old and, according to a 2011 Congressional Research Service report, with limited budgetary resources and aging infrastructure, Reclamation's maintenance needs are likely to increase, as is competition for limited funding.[24]

Despite the ongoing challenges of operating and maintaining aging infrastructure under budgetary constraints, it is important that the Corps and Reclamation address the challenge of managing climate change risk in order to limit the fiscal exposure of the federal government. As noted in our 2013 high-risk update, climate change poses a significant financial risk to the federal government, including, but not limited to its role as the owner or operator of extensive infrastructure vulnerable to climate impacts. State and local authorities are responsible for planning and implementing many types of infrastructure projects, and decisions at these levels of government can affect the federal government's fiscal

[22]L.D. Brekke, J.E. Kiang, J.R. Olsen, R.S. Pulwarty, D.A. Raff, D.P. Turnipseed, R.S. Webb, and K.D. White, *Climate change and water resources management—A federal perspective: USGS Circular 1331(2009).*

[23]Committee on U.S. Army Corps of Engineers Water Resources Science, Engineering, and Planning; Water Science and Technology Board; Division on Earth and Life Studies; National Research Council, *Corps of Engineers Water Resources Infrastructure: Deterioration, Investment, or Divestment?* (The National Academies Press, Washington, D.C.: 2012).

[24]Congressional Research Service, *The Bureau of Reclamation's Aging Infrastructure,* March 30, 2011.

GAO-14-23 Climate Change Adaptation

exposure.[25] While implementing adaptive strategies to protect infrastructure may be costly, there is a growing recognition that the cost of inaction could be greater and—given the government's precarious fiscal position—increasingly difficult to manage given expected budget pressures, which will constrain not just future ad hoc responses, but other federal programs as well. As stated in a 2010 National Research Council report, increasing the nation's ability to respond to a changing climate can be viewed as an insurance policy against climate change risks.[26]

Efforts Under Way by the Corps and Reclamation to Assess Water Resource and Infrastructure Vulnerabilities to Climate Change and Develop Adaptation Strategies

Since 2009, as directed by executive order or required by law, the Corps and Reclamation have taken steps to assess water resource and infrastructure vulnerabilities and develop guidance and strategies for adapting to climate change, as shown in table 2.[27] Officials from both agencies told us that as they develop the necessary guidance, they plan to implement specific adaptation strategies and share costs with state and local partners.

---

[25]The federal government annually invests billions of dollars in infrastructure projects that state and local governments prioritize and supervise through, for example, decisions on zoning and how to build vulnerable infrastructure such as roads and bridges. See GAO-10-113.

[26]National Research Council, *America's Climate Choices: Adapting to the Impacts of Climate Change* (Washington, D.C.: 2010).

[27]Other activities to address adaptation challenges, such as the development of new climate and hydrologic projections, computer tools to work with the projections, websites to facilitate user access to these resources, and training programs for on-the-ground water resources practitioners, are discussed later in this report.

Table 1: Corps and Reclamation Efforts to Assess Climate Change Vulnerabilities and Develop Adaptation Strategies and Guidance

Activities	Corps	Reclamation
Assessing climate change vulnerabilities	Completed: High-level assessment of climate change impacts on agency missions and operations. Ongoing: Conducting an initial assessment of climate change impact vulnerability for coastal activities. Developing and testing methodologies for assessing climate impacts at the watershed level for inland activities and a separate methodology for coastal activities.	Completed: High-level assessment of climate change impacts on water supplies in the major river basins in the West. Ongoing: Assessment of climate change impacts to water demands, including agricultural demands.
Developing adaptation strategies and guidance	Ongoing: Conducting pilot studies to support the development of adaptation guidance and a portfolio of adaptation approaches. Developing guidance for considering adaptation in all agency activities and for the implementation of adaptation approaches.	Ongoing: Conducting more focused assessments within basins to develop strategies to mitigate climate change impacts on water supplies. Developing guidance for considering adaptation in specific agency activities.

Sources: GAO analysis of Corps and Reclamation information.

The Corps Completed a Mission-Level Vulnerability Assessment and Is Conducting Pilot Studies to Identify Adaptation Strategies

Since 2009, the Corps has broadly assessed how climate change could affect its missions. Specifically, a phased assessment of the vulnerability of coastal projects is under way, more refined watershed-level vulnerability assessments are being developed, and pilot studies are being conducted to develop adaptation guidance and strategies. In March 2012, responding to guidance for implementing Executive Order 13514, the Corps provided the President's Council on Environmental Quality with a high-level analysis of the vulnerability of the Corps' missions and operations to climate change.[28] The Corps' analysis included an assessment of whether the potential effects of climate change on the Corps' business areas would likely be negative, positive, or a mix of both.[29] The analysis found, for example, that increasing air temperatures may have an effect on glaciers that could negatively impact Corps

---

[28]The Corps included excerpts of this assessment in its June 2012 *Climate Adaptation Plan and Report*, provided to the Council on Environmental Quality as required by Executive Order 13514.

[29]Corps business areas cover the following: navigation, flood and coastal storm damage reduction, environment, hydropower, regulatory, recreation, emergency management, and water supply.

business areas such as navigation, flood and coastal storm damage reduction, ecosystem restoration, and emergency management, but the effect of increasing air temperatures on river ice could have both positive and negative impacts on those same four business areas.

As part of the high-level analysis, the Corps also identified a number of adaptation priorities. To address its priority of developing more refined vulnerability assessments, the Corps is currently undertaking coastal project vulnerability assessments and is developing and testing a methodology for nationwide, watershed-level vulnerability assessments of its inland missions, operations, programs, and projects. The nationwide watershed-level vulnerability assessments will, according to Corps officials, help them make initial screening-level determinations of where adaptation strategies are needed or not needed, and then to prioritize accordingly. The agency officials expect to complete the first phase of screening assessments in 2013, with more refined assessments to come in future years. Ultimately, the Corps plans to combine the coastal and inland assessments into a unified methodology. In addition, Corps Civil Works officials told us that they are developing syntheses of literature to provide up-to-date information about regional climate impacts in order to support project-specific planning and help implement adaptation strategies.

As part of its efforts to address the adaptation priorities of developing a risk-informed decision-making framework for climate change adaptation and a portfolio of adaptation approaches, the Corps is conducting 15 pilot studies nationwide to test different methods and frameworks for adapting to climate change. The Corps has completed 5 of these studies and 10 others are ongoing.[30] According to Corps Civil Works officials, the pilot studies were proposed by Corps district staff and selected by senior Corps staff in a competitive, internal process. The 15 pilots are led by 13 different Corps districts and address project planning, engineering, operations, and maintenance for 6 different Corps business areas, involving a variety of different infrastructure types, such as flood risk reduction projects, reservoirs, and canals. Some of the pilots are being conducted collaboratively with federal, state, and university partners. Taken together, Corps officials expect the pilot projects to provide a body of knowledge and tested methods that will serve as the foundation for its

---

[30]The Corps plans to initiate one additional pilot in 2013.

guidance and future adaptation efforts. See appendix II for additional information on the locations and results of the Corps' pilot studies.

Reclamation Assessed Vulnerabilities in Major Western River Basins and Is Developing Potential Adaptation Strategies

Reclamation has broadly assessed how climate change may affect water resources in the western United States as part of the Basin Study Program it established to meet the requirements of the SECURE Water Act. Specifically, responding to the Act's requirement to assess specific risks to water supplies,[31] Reclamation reported to Congress in 2011 its assessments of the potential effects of climate change on water supplies in the major river basins in the West.[32] The studies, known as West-Wide Climate Risk Assessments (WWCRA), are high-level, baseline assessments of the potential impacts of climate change on future water supplies—including impacts on Reclamation's ability to deliver water and hydropower—for each of the major river basins where Reclamation owns and operates water management infrastructure. According to agency officials, Reclamation is now conducting WWCRAs that focus on future water demand and will combine this information with its water supply assessments to form a more complete picture of the potential impacts of climate change on its water infrastructure.[33] Reclamation policy officials told us that these combined assessments will be included in Reclamation's next SECURE Water Act report that is due in 2016. These assessments will also be updated based on the latest climate science as water uses and conditions change, and they will be included in future reports that are due to Congress every 5 years.[34]

In addition to its WWCRAs, Reclamation is partnering with nonfederal entities to conduct more focused assessments, known as Basin Studies, to identify specific water resources vulnerabilities and to implement the SECURE Water Act's requirement that Reclamation consider and develop strategies to mitigate climate change impacts on water

---

[31]Pub. L. No. 111-11, § 9503(b)(2) (2009).

[32]The SECURE Water Act identifies eight major reclamation river basins, but Reclamation only conducted seven West-Wide Climate Risk Assessments because one covers both the Sacramento and San Joaquin River Basins.

[33]Reclamation officials told us the assessments are meant to fulfill the requirements of section 9503(b)(3) of the SECURE Water Act.

[34]Pub. L. No. 111-11, § 9503(c) (2009).

supplies.[35] Reclamation selects the Basin Studies through a competitive process and shares their costs with nonfederal partners. Through the Basin Studies, Reclamation intends to identify basin-wide water supply vulnerabilities, project climate change's impacts on the performance of water infrastructure, and develop adaptation strategies—such as operational or physical changes to existing water infrastructure or development of new facilities—to address these impacts. According to Reclamation guidance, the Basin Studies are to develop long-term projections of water supply and demand that take into account specific climate change risks identified in the SECURE Water Act.[36] The studies will analyze how well existing water and power infrastructure are meeting current demands and then forecast their performance in light of projected water supply and demand. To address projected imbalances in supply and demand, the studies are to identify adaptation strategies that include strategies for nonstructural (i.e., management and operations) and structural (i.e., capital expenditures) changes.

As of September 2013, 3 Basin Studies have been completed, and an additional 14 studies have been funded and are under way.[37] Reclamation and its partners, including state water management agencies and local irrigation districts, completed the Yakima River Basin Study in 2011, and both the St. Mary River and Milk River Basins Study and Colorado River Basin Study in 2012. Some studies entirely cover the major river basins specified in the SECURE Water Act—such as the Colorado River Basin Study, while other studies cover subbasins or tributaries within the boundaries of the major river basins—such as the Yakima River Basin Study, covering a tributary of the Columbia River. Reclamation officials told us that they next intend to initiate feasibility studies for adaptation strategies identified in completed Basin Studies by making funds available to nonfederal partners, beginning with an initial feasibility study in 2013. See appendix II for additional information on the locations and results of Reclamation's Basin Studies.

---

[35]Pub. L. No. 111-11, § 9503(b)(4) (2009).

[36]Pub. L. No. 111-11, § 9503(b)(2) (2009).

[37]Two additional studies were selected for funding in fiscal year 2013.

Both Agencies Are Developing and Enhancing Guidance for Implementing Climate Adaptation Strategies Identified

As recommended by the Task Force in 2010, the Corps and Reclamation are taking a phased approach to climate adaptation, including developing agency-wide guidance for adaptation. Specifically, through broad climate vulnerability assessments, agency officials told us they have expanded their knowledge of climate change and its impacts, allowing them to assess, at a high level, how these impacts may affect agency missions, programs, and operations. These initial vulnerability assessments have informed the agencies in developing and conducting more detailed vulnerability assessments, while also identifying specific strategies for climate change adaptation through the pilots and basin studies. Both agencies have also begun integrating what they have learned into their policies and program guidance. For example, beginning in 2009 and updated in 2011, the Corps issued guidance requiring that potential sea-level changes be considered in all of the agency's coastal planning, engineering, operations, and maintenance activities. The Corps is currently developing guidance for implementing coastal and inland adaptation strategies. Similarly, in 2013, Reclamation officials told us they began to incorporate climate change adaptation considerations into its policies and guidance for project feasibility studies and environmental impact studies, among other things, using information and lessons learned from its WWCRA and Basin Study vulnerability assessments.

According to agency officials, as the Corps and Reclamation integrate climate adaptation considerations into their policies and program guidance, they will begin to take steps toward implementing the potential adaptation strategies that they have identified. According to the Corps' 2012 adaptation plan, the agency's goal is to create a policy and guidance framework that will support the implementation of practical, nationally consistent, legally justifiable, and cost-effective adaptation strategies. Accordingly, Corps Civil Works officials told us that the pilots conducted to date have been largely focused on informing the development of policy and guidance, and that no structural or operational adaptation strategies have been implemented. Similarly, Reclamation officials told us no structural or operational adaptation strategies have been implemented in response to the agency's vulnerability assessments, and that its efforts to update guidance will be informed by the adaptation strategy feasibility studies as they are completed.

Corps and Reclamation officials told us that because they are early in the adaptation process, the extent to which limited budgets and existing infrastructure maintenance backlogs will affect the implementation of adaptation strategies remains to be determined. However, the implementation of adaptation strategies by both agencies will likely rely on collaborative sharing of costs and resources with federal, state, local, and nongovernmental stakeholders. Both agencies have already initiated cost-sharing and resource-leveraging measures. For example, according to agency officials, the Corps is leveraging resources for adaptation pilot studies with state, local, and nongovernmental entities, and Reclamation is splitting the cost of Basin Studies with state and local partners. The agencies plan to continue such collaborative approaches going forward. For example, as required under the SECURE Water Act, Reclamation officials told us they intend to share the cost of the feasibility studies for adaptation strategies equally with nonfederal partners.

The Corps and Reclamation Face Several Challenges in Assessing and Responding to the Effects of Climate Change and Are Working Collaboratively to Address Them

In 2009, the Corps and Reclamation—with its CCAWWG partners NOAA and USGS—published a study,[38] (referred to in this report as the CCAWWG study). This study identified several challenges that climate change poses for water resource managers, including (1) identifying the data and tools needed by water managers to address climate change, (2) ensuring the sustained collection of climate data, (3) incorporating climate science into water management tools, and (4) educating water managers to use climate data and tools. We found that the Corps and Reclamation are addressing these challenges, making collaboration a key element of their efforts, and doing so in a manner generally consistent with best practices for sustained collaboration.

The Corps and Reclamation Are Addressing Several Challenges to Climate Adaptation

The CCAWWG study identified a number of challenges faced by the Corps and Reclamation in adapting to climate change, and the agencies have taken a variety of actions to address these challenges.

- *Identifying the data and tools needed by water managers to address climate change:* The CCAWWG agencies are collaborating to produce a series of four documents identifying their common data and tool needs and a strategy for meeting them, with the objective, among

---

[38]L.D. Brekke, J.E. Kiang, J.R. Olsen, R.S. Pulwarty, D.A. Raff, D.P. Turnipseed, R.S. Webb, and K.D. White, *Climate change and water resources management—A federal perspective: USGS Circular 1331 (2009).*

other things, of guiding and fostering federal and nonfederal research and technology investments toward meeting these needs.[39] The first document, published in 2011, described the water management community's needs for climate change information and tools to support long-term planning for time scales of 5 years and more. The second document, published in 2013, described the data and tools needed to support short-term planning of less than 5 years. For both documents, the Corps and Reclamation asked their water resource managers to identify the information and tools most relevant to their programs, and they also consulted with other federal, state, and local agencies and stakeholders with a role in water resource management about their needs. The documents summarized the information and tools needed into categories and identified the users' most pressing needs within each category. According to these documents, the CCAWWG agencies plan next to prepare two companion documents to identify a scientific strategy for meeting the research needs identified in the two initial documents. The two completed documents note that USGS and NOAA will jointly prepare the companion documents, incorporating perspectives from other federal and nonfederal representatives of the scientific community.

- *Ensuring the sustained collection of climate data:* The Corps and Reclamation are coordinating with the data collecting agencies and sharing some costs associated with their efforts. According to the 2009 CCAWWG study, at the same time as the need for observational data to support climate adaptation is increasing, the observational networks crucial to increasing understanding are shrinking. For example, in recent decades, maintenance of long-term monitoring networks has declined because of a lack of funding—USGS alone has deactivated or discontinued almost 1,700 surface-water stream gauges. Corps Civil Works officials told us that stream gauge data is extremely important, not only to the Corps' ongoing operations, but also because science agencies use the data to produce the climate change information upon which the Corps bases its adaptation planning. To ensure the needed data is collected, the Corps has a

---

[39]*Addressing Climate Change in Long-Term Water Resources Planning and Management: User Needs for Improving Tools and Information,* U.S. Army Corps of Engineers and U.S. Department of the Interior, Bureau of Reclamation (Washington D.C.: January 2011) and *Short-Term Water Management Decisions: User Needs for Improved Climate, Weather, and Hydrologic Information,* U.S. Army Corps of Engineers, Bureau of Reclamation, and NOAA (Washington D.C.: January 2013).

formal agreement to provide funding to USGS—about $18 million in fiscal year 2013 according to Corps officials—to operate stream gauges that provide data for the Corps' water planning and management activities. This data is also available for use by all federal and state agencies, as well as others interested in water information.

Reclamation policy officials told us, in response to a SECURE Water Act requirement to consult with federal and applicable state agencies to develop a monitoring plan for acquiring and maintaining water resources information, agency staff are currently identifying information needs and plans to work collaboratively with data collecting agencies, including NOAA, USGS, and the U.S. Department of Agriculture, to develop the plan.[40] Reclamation policy officials stated that the Basin Study Program activities, including the WWCRAs and Basin Studies, are also contributing to the planning effort by providing valuable information about how the agency's monitoring needs are changing as a result of climate change. Reclamation officials told us that they intend to work with the U.S. Department of Agriculture and USGS to initiate the required monitoring plan in 2014. These collaborative efforts can help ensure that the long-term water resource monitoring networks critical for detecting and quantifying climate change and its impacts—as well as measuring the effectiveness of future adaptation strategies—will be properly configured and continue to operate.

- *Incorporating climate science into water management tools:* The Corps, Reclamation, and others are collaborating in a number of efforts to incorporate climate science into water management tools.[41]

---

[40]We found in previous reports that gaps in NOAA's satellite coverage, which could occur as soon as 2014, are expected to affect the continuity of climate and space weather measurements. Given the importance of satellite data to weather forecasts, the likelihood of significant gaps, and the potential impact of such gaps on the health and safety of the U.S. population and economy, GAO has concluded that the potential gap in weather satellite data is a high-risk area and added it to the High-Risk List in 2013. For example, see GAO, *Environmental Satellites: Focused Attention Needed to Mitigate Program Risks*, GAO-12-841T (Washington, D.C.: June 27, 2012). See also GAO, *Environmental Satellites: Strategy Needed to Sustain Critical Climate and Space Weather Measurements*, GAO-10-456 (Washington, D.C.: Apr. 27, 2010).

[41]In our 2013 High-Risk Update, we identified the need to develop a government-wide approach for providing (1) the best available climate-related data for making decisions at the state and local level and (2) assistance for translating available climate-related data into information that officials need to make decisions.

For example, Reclamation research and development, as well as policy officials told us that as part of their effort to enhance the capabilities of water resource managers to use climate data, the agency is coleading two of Interior's Landscape Conservation Cooperatives in the Colorado River Basin area. Reclamation officials told us that the Landscape Conservation Cooperatives, which are partnerships of governmental and nongovernmental stakeholders, will focus on developing and communicating science to inform climate adaptation strategies for ecological regions, or "landscapes." In collaboration with academia, other federal agencies, local and state partners, and the public, the Landscape Conservation Cooperatives will provide products and services, such as climate change computer models and vulnerability assessments, coordinate with Interior's regional Climate Science Centers to synthesize existing climate change impact data and management strategies, and help resource managers put them into action on the ground.[42] The Landscape Conservation Cooperatives will also coordinate with NOAA's Regional Integrated Sciences and Assessment program.[43]

Similarly, the Corps is engaged in collaborative efforts with external partners to integrate climate science into planning tools for water resource managers. For example, the Corps partnered with NOAA's National Ocean Service to create an online sea level change calculator. According to Corps officials, this collaboration allowed the rapid integration of climate science into engineering guidance for coastal projects. Corps Civil Works officials also told us that collaboration with the Federal Emergency Management Agency and NOAA's Urban Northeast Regional Integrated Sciences and Assessment program contributed to the development of a post-Superstorm Sandy sea level rise tool to help affected communities,

---

[42]Interior's eight regional Climate Science Centers deliver basic climate change impact science to Landscape Conservation Cooperatives within their respective regions, including physical and biological research, ecological forecasting, and multiscale modeling. The centers prioritize their delivery of fundamental science, data, and decision-support activities to meet the needs of the Landscape Conservation Cooperatives

[43]The Regional Integrated Sciences and Assessment program consists of 11 research teams that emphasize collaborative regional climate research to help inform climate change adaptation planning and management.

residents, and other stakeholders consider risks from future sea level rise in planning for reconstruction.[44]

In addition, the Corps and NOAA are coleading actions to implement the Task Force recommendation to develop a federal Internet portal to provide current, relevant, and high-quality information on water resources and climate change data applications and tools for assessing the vulnerability of water programs and facilities to climate change. As a result, the Corps-hosted Federal Support Toolbox is now publicly available online. According to Corps Civil Works officials, the website is a "one stop shop" for technical resources to support water management. The website states that the Toolbox is an evolving and comprehensive water resources data portal with direct links to valuable databases, innovative programs and initiatives, and state-of-the-art models and tools.[45]

- *Educating water managers to use climate data and tools:* The Corps and Reclamation are collaborating as coleaders in developing and implementing a training program as recommended by the Task Force's *National Action Plan: Priorities for Managing Freshwater Resources in a Changing Environment*.[46] These agencies—joined by NOAA, USGS, and the Environmental Protection Agency—are collaborating with the University Corporation for Atmospheric Research's COMET Program and the Western Water Assessment to produce training courses for federal and nonfederal resource management professionals who need to assess the impacts of climate

---

[44]In 2012, Superstorm Sandy caused tens of billions of dollars in damages to buildings, utilities, transportation systems, and other infrastructure. As we pointed out in our 2013 High-Risk Update, as weather-related events become more frequent and intense due to climate change, whatever resulting damages are not covered by insurance or built to be resilient to such events increases the federal government's implicit fiscal exposure through federal disaster relief programs.

[45]The Federal Support Toolbox is available at www.watertoolbox.us

[46]According to the CCAWWG study, adaptation to climate change will likely require water resource managers to move away from the traditional planning assumption of stationarity—the idea that historical records of stream flow and weather variation represent a reasonable proxy for the future—in designing and operating water resource systems. In the absence of stationarity, water managers will need to use new methods to estimate the likelihood of future hydrologic conditions, including approaches that use climate models to project a range of possible future condition scenarios.

change on water and related resources.[47] Specifically, in 2012, the agencies implemented an online course on incorporating climate change into water resource planning, which was a prerequisite for participating in the first two pilot residence courses—addressing climate impacts on surface hydrology and on water demand for irrigated crops—offered in early 2013. According to the program's website, the online course was designed to provide students with water resource planning knowledge, while the residence courses offer opportunities for gaining hands-on experience in applying that knowledge. According to the website, these courses and the numerous planned future classes are collectively designed to provide a professional development and training series that will help managers assess climate change impacts across the spectrum of natural resources.

The Corps' and Reclamation's Collaborative Efforts Are Generally Consistent with the Best Practices for Enhanced and Sustained Collaboration

The Corps and Reclamation have collaborated with each other and other agencies in a manner that is generally consistent with practices that we have previously identified as important to helping enhance and sustain collaboration among federal agencies.[48] In 2005, we reported that collaboration—broadly defined as any joint activity that is intended to produce more public value than could be produced when organizations act alone—can be enhanced and sustained by engaging in eight key practices: (1) defining and articulating a common outcome; (2) establishing mutually reinforcing or joint strategies; (3) identifying and addressing needs by leveraging resources; (4) agreeing on roles and responsibilities; (5) establishing compatible policies, procedures, and other means to operate across agency boundaries; (6) developing mechanisms to monitor, evaluate, and report on results; (7) reinforcing agency accountability for collaborative efforts through agency plans and

---

[47]The University Corporation for Atmospheric Research is a consortium of over 100 member universities and academic affiliates focused on research and training in the atmospheric and related earth system sciences. Its COMET Program uses innovative methods to disseminate and enhance scientific knowledge in the environmental sciences, particularly meteorology, but also including diverse areas such as oceanography, hydrology, space weather, and emergency management. The Western Water Assessment is a university-based applied research program that addresses societal vulnerabilities related to climate, particularly in the area of water resources. Its mission is to identify and characterize regional vulnerabilities to and impacts of climate variability and change and to develop information, products, and processes to assist decision makers throughout Colorado, Utah, and Wyoming.

[48]GAO-06-15.

reports; and (8) reinforcing individual accountability for collaborative efforts through performance management systems. Running throughout these practices are a number of factors, such as leadership, trust, and organizational culture, which are necessary elements for a collaborative working relationship.

The Corps and Reclamation have made collaboration a key element of their adaptation policies and plans and have reinforced accountability for collaboration through agency performance management systems. For example, the Corps' climate adaptation policy states that collaborations are the most effective way to develop strategies to identify and reduce vulnerabilities to potential future climate change, and it calls for continued collaborative adaptation efforts. As stated in the Corps' 2012 *Climate Adaptation Plan and Report*, it is the objective of the agency to facilitate and promote closer and more fruitful interagency cooperation and to promote sharing of impact and adaptation data and information between federal, state, and local partners. Finally, to reinforce accountability, the draft performance metrics for climate adaptation in the Corps' 2013 *Army Campaign Plan* includes a target for the number of products developed in collaboration with other water resource agencies for adaptation planning and action.

Reclamation has similarly included collaboration as a key element of its adaptation policy, plans, and performance metrics. Under Interior's 2013 Climate Change Adaptation Policy, Reclamation is to integrate climate change adaptation strategies into its policies and practices by, among other actions, collaborating with stakeholders through Landscape Conservation Cooperatives, Climate Science Centers, and other partnerships to increase understanding of climate change. Furthermore, Reclamation's strategic plan for its adaptation and conservation programs states that collaborative partnerships must be developed to identify the adaptive strategies needed to address climate change. Finally, through its climate adaptation efforts, Reclamation is contributing to Interior's goal of identifying resources that are particularly vulnerable to climate change and implementing coordinated adaptation responses for half of the nation by September 30, 2013.

We also found that the Corps and Reclamation have collaborated together and with others in accordance with best practices for collaboration among agencies. For example, in their key collaborative effort—CCAWWG—each agency's role is well defined; the Corps and Reclamation provide water engineering and management expertise, and their partner agencies provide climate science expertise. CCAWWG has clearly defined common objectives, including the development of working level relationships between federal water management and federal science agencies, and it leverages resources across agencies to meet common needs. The CCAWWG agencies also have mutually reinforcing strategies. For example, the operating needs of the Corps and Reclamation drive the direction of science inquiries by the science agencies, resulting in improved operations, while at the same time the data collected and compiled by the water management agencies for a specific purpose can be used by the science agencies for alternative objectives. Outside of CCAWWG, as mentioned elsewhere in this report, the agencies have also followed key collaborative practices, such as the Corps leveraging resources to fund maintenance of the USGS's stream-flow monitoring networks, and Reclamation establishing joint strategies with state agencies and others to conduct Basin Studies.

Agency Comments

We provided a draft of this product for review and comment to the Departments of Defense and the Interior. The Department of Defense provided technical comments that were incorporated, as appropriate.

As agreed with your offices, unless you publicly announce the contents of this report earlier, we plan no further distribution until 30 days from the report date. At that time we will send copies to the Secretaries of Defense and the Interior; the appropriate congressional committees; and other interested parties. In addition, the report will be available at no charge on the GAO website at http://www.gao.gov.

If you or your staff members have questions about this report, please contact me at (202) 512-3841 or morriss@gao.gov. Contact points for our Offices of Congressional Relations and Public Affairs may be found on the last page of this report. GAO staff who made key contributions to this report are listed in appendix III.

Steve D. Morris
Acting Director, Natural Resources and Environment

Appendix I: The U.S. Army Corps of Engineers' and the Bureau of Reclamation's Organization and Infrastructure

The U.S. Army Corps of Engineers (Corps)—an agency within the Department of Defense and a Major Command within the Army—is composed of four program areas including Civil Works, Military Construction, Real Estate, and Research and Development. To carry out its Civil Works missions nationwide, the program is organized into eight geographic divisions composed of 38 districts, as shown in figure 1. Division and district geographic boundaries are generally aligned with watershed boundaries.

Figure 1: U.S. Army Corps of Engineers Division and District Boundaries

Sources: U.S. Army Corps of Engineers, Map Resources (map).

Note: In addition to the eight divisions that manage U.S. water resources, the Corps also operates a Gulf Region Division, Afghanistan Engineer District, and Europe District.

The Corps' Civil Works Program is implemented through nine business areas that represent the diversity of the nation's water resource management needs as follows:

- Navigation—provides safe and reliable commercial waterways;
- Flood and Coastal Storm Damage Reduction—reduces risks to people, homes, and communities from flooding and coastal storms;
- Environment—restores and protects wetlands and other aquatic ecosystems;
- Hydropower—generates hydroelectric power for distribution to communities;
- Regulatory—regulates work in navigable rivers and the discharge of dredges and fill materials in U.S. waters;
- Recreation—provides recreational and educational opportunities;
- Emergency Management—prepares for natural disasters and acts when they occur;
- Water Supply—provides water storage for multiple purposes; and
- Executive Direction and Management—provides leadership, strategic planning and performance measurement.

To implement its responsibilities in the business areas, the Corps has constructed—and continues to operate, maintain, and rehabilitate—a large inventory and wide variety of water management infrastructure. For example, according to Corps records, as of September 2012, its inventory includes 702 reservoirs that, among other things, provide water supply storage and help reduce flood risk, and 75 hydropower facilities with 353 generating units that produce hydroelectric power for homes, businesses, and communities. In the area of navigation, the Corps' inventory includes 12,000 miles of commercial inland waterways, 193 lock sites with 239 chambers, and 926 harbors.[1] For flood reduction, the Corps inventory includes 14,501 miles of levee systems. For recreation, the Corps' inventory includes 54,879 miles of lakeshore and recreation areas that support 370 million annual visitors, 270,000 jobs, and $16 billion of economic activity. In 2012, the National Research Council reported that the Corps' infrastructure had an estimated value of approximately $164 billion.

The Department of the Interior's Bureau of Reclamation (Reclamation) is, according to agency records, the nation's largest wholesale water supplier, providing water to over 31 million people and irrigation water to one out of five western farmers on 10 million acres of farm land, which produce 60 percent of the nation's vegetables and one-quarter of its fresh

---

[1] A lock is a navigation device with one or more fixed chambers in which the water level can be varied, allowing the raising and lowering of boats between stretches of water of different levels on rivers and canals.

fruit and nut crops. Reclamation is also the second largest producer of hydropower in the United States. To carry out its mission and operations, Reclamation is organized into five regions, as shown in figure 1.

Figure 2: Bureau of Reclamation Regional Boundaries

Sources: U.S. Bureau of Reclamation, Map Resources (map).

According to agency records as of 2011, Reclamation's asset inventory includes 476 dams and dikes, creating 337 reservoirs with a total storage capacity of 245 million acre-feet of water.[2] Reclamation's inventory also includes 53 hydroelectric power plants that it owns and operates. These plants provide an average of more than 40 megawatt hours of energy per year.[3] In 2011, Reclamation, estimated that the replacement value of its assets was approximately $90 billion. According to the Congressional Research Service, about two-thirds of the assets in Reclamation's inventory are "transferred works"—facilities that it owns, but for which it has transferred operations and maintenance to nonfederal entities. The remaining one-third of these facilities are "reserved works"—facilities that are owned, operated, and maintained by Reclamation, where the nonfederal beneficiaries, such as irrigation districts, are responsible for repaying construction and maintenance costs.

---

[2]An acre-foot is 325,851 gallons of water that, according to Reclamation, supplies enough water for a family of four for 1 year.

[3]A megawatt hour is one thousand kilowatt-hours or one million watt-hours, which will power the average American home for 1 week.

Appendix II: Locations and Initial Results of the U.S. Army Corps of Engineer's Pilot Studies and Bureau of Reclamation's Basin Studies

The Corps is conducting pilot studies nationwide to support the development of adaptation guidance and a portfolio of adaptation approaches. Reclamation is conducting Basin Studies—focused assessments within basins—to develop strategies to mitigate climate change impacts on water supplies.

Corps Pilot Studies

As part of its efforts to address the priorities of developing a risk-informed decision-making framework and a portfolio of adaptation approaches, the Corps is conducting 15 pilot studies nationwide to test different methods and frameworks for adapting to climate change (see fig. 3). As of September 2013, the Corps has completed 5 of these studies, and 10 others are ongoing. The Corps plans to initiate 1 additional pilot in 2013.

Appendix II: Locations and Initial Results of
the U.S. Army Corps of Engineer's Pilot
Studies and Bureau of Reclamation's Basin
Studies

Figure 3: Location and Description of U.S. Army Corps of Engineers Pilot Projects, as of September 2013

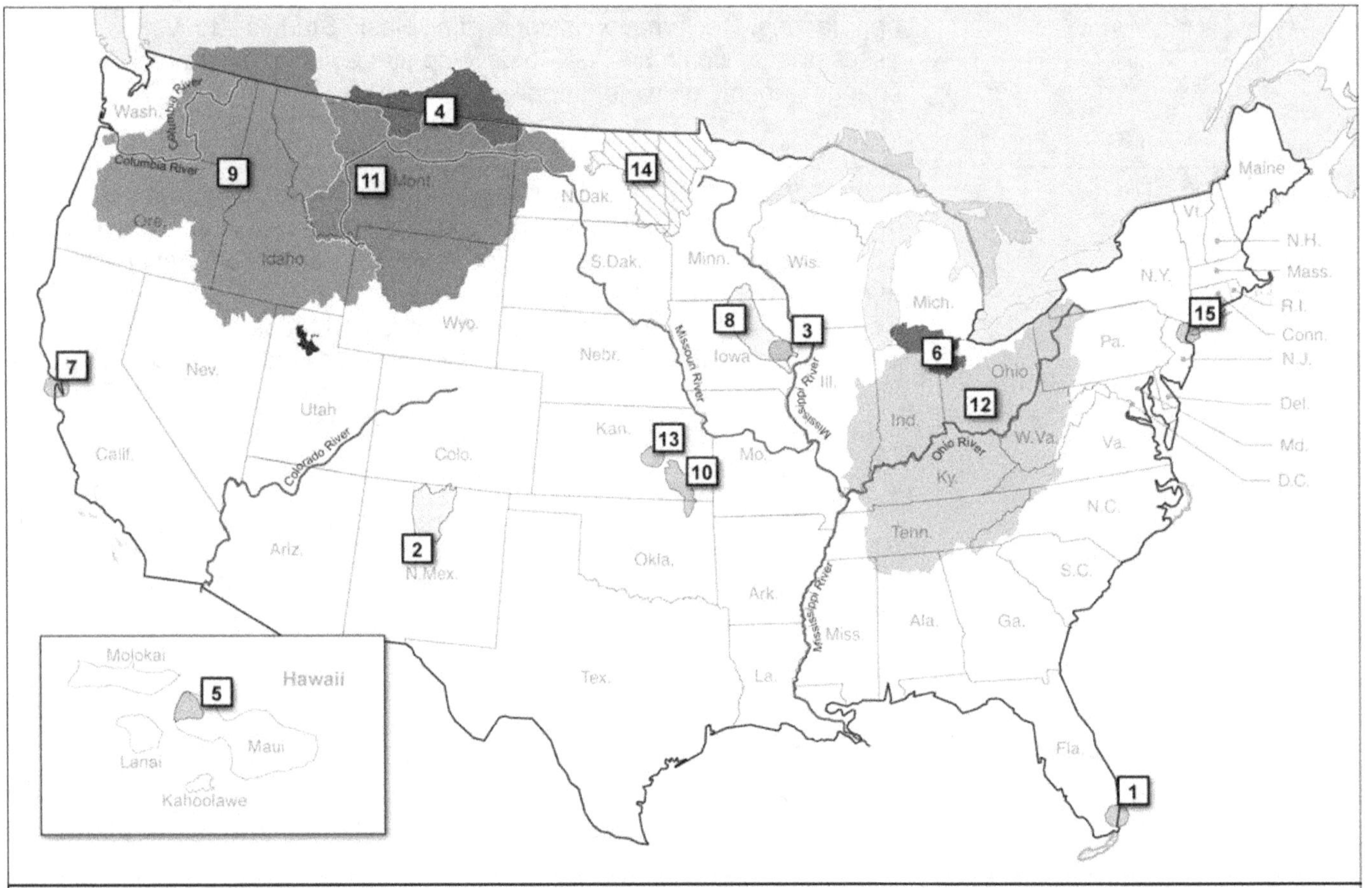

1 Application of Sea-Level Change Guidance to C-111 Spreader Canal, Florida

2 Climate Change Associated Sediment Yield Impacts on the Rio Grande, Cochiti Dam and Lake

3 Climate Change Impacts on the Operation of Coralville Lake, Iowa

4 Climate Change Associated Sediment Yield Impacts and Operation Evaluations at Garrison Dam, North Dakota

5 Risk-Informed Decision-Making for Integrated Water Resource Management Planning, West Maui Watershed

6 Upland Sediment Production and Delivery in the Great Lakes Region under Climate Change

7 Risk-Informed Decision-Making for Potential Sea-Level Rise Impacts on the Hamilton Wetland Restoration Project, California

8 Climate Modeling and Stakeholder Engagement to Support Adaptation in the Iowa-Cedar Watershed

9 Framework for Building Resiliency into Restoration Planning – Lower Columbia River Estuary

10 Climate Change Impacts on Water Supply in Marion Reservoir Watershed, Kansas

11 Missouri River Basin Mountain Snowpack – Accumulation and Runoff

12 Formulating Mitigation/Adaptation Strategies through Regional Collaboration with the Ohio River Basin Alliance

13 Utilization of Regional Climate Science Programs in Reservoir and Watershed Risk-Based Assessments, Oologah Lake and Watershed

14 Red River of the North Flooding at Fargo, North Dakota

15 East Rockaway Inlet to Rockaway Inlet, New York, Collaboration Framework Development

Sources: U.S. Army Corps of Engineers, Map Resources (map).

Note: Pilot studies 1-5 have been completed as of September 2013.

Appendix II: Locations and Initial Results of
the U.S. Army Corps of Engineer's Pilot
Studies and Bureau of Reclamation's Basin
Studies

According to the Corps' September 2012 report on its climate change adaptation pilots,[1] each study addresses a central question designed to help the Corps, according to officials, test new ideas, develop and utilize information at the project-level scale, and to collect information needed to develop policy and guidance for incorporating adaptation into all agency activities. For example, because the reliability of a planned flood reduction project could depend on how climate change affects future flooding, the Corps launched a pilot study with the goals of determining (1) whether tools and data are available for the Corps to provide reliable estimates of future flooding using climate projections and (2) how changes in precipitation patterns will affect flood events. This pilot study's results supports the Corps' effort to design an approximately $1.8 billion flood risk reduction project on the Red River of the North, where flooding has increased in magnitude and frequency since 1942. According to Corps officials, the pilot study successfully adapted existing tools and data to project future flooding, while also testing current guidance and contributing to the development of new guidance for future adaptation efforts. Specifically, Corps officials told us that climate data indicated a trend of flooding consistent with climate change projections. In accordance with existing Corps risk analysis guidance, the pilot study leader convened an expert panel to review the climate information. Based on the expert panel's findings, the pilot team is integrating climate data into the Corps' flood model to project future river conditions. In addition, a member of the pilot study team who is also responsible for developing the Corps' guidance for inland adaptation activities told us that he is integrating his observations and experiences from this study—as well as from his participation in other Corps pilots—into the guidance.

Corps officials told us that the information developed by the Corps' climate change adaptation pilots is also contributing to subsequent Corps studies. For example, the climate change and modeling data for a pilot study of sediment impacts to Cochiti Dam and Lake in New Mexico is contributing to ongoing studies in the Corps' Albuquerque District. One is the Santa Clara Pueblo Watershed Assessment, which is studying observed climate trends and projected climate changes to address likely future changes to watershed hydrology on the Pueblo's lands, with particular attention to flood risk and water resources development.

---

[1]U.S. Army Corps of Engineers, *Climate Change Adaptation Pilots* (June 2012).

Appendix II: Locations and Initial Results of
the U.S. Army Corps of Engineer's Pilot
Studies and Bureau of Reclamation's Basin
Studies

Reclamation Basin Studies

Reclamation is partnering with nonfederal entities to conduct focused assessments, known as Basin Studies, to identify specific water resources vulnerabilities and to implement the SECURE Water Act's requirement that Reclamation consider and develop strategies to mitigate climate change impacts on water supplies.[2] As of September 2013, 3 Basin Studies have been completed, and an additional 14 studies have been funded and are under way in western states (see fig. 4).[3]

---

[2]Pub. L. No. 111-11, § 9503(b)(4) (2009).

[3]Two additional studies were selected for funding in fiscal year 2013: the San Diego Watershed Basin Study and the West Salt River Valley Basin Study. Reclamation is developing the scopes of the studies with the respective funding partners.

Appendix II: Locations and Initial Results of
the U.S. Army Corps of Engineer's Pilot
Studies and Bureau of Reclamation's Basin
Studies

Figure 4: Locations of the Bureau of Reclamation's 17 Funded Basin Studies, as of September 2013

	Basin Study name	Year initiated
1	Colorado River Basin Water Supply and Demand Study	2009
2	St. Mary River and Milk River Basins Study	2009
3	Yakima River Basin Study	2009
4	Henrys Fork of the Snake River Basin Study	2010
5	Niobrara River Basin Study	2010
6	Santa Ana River Watershed Basin Study	2010
7	Southeast California Regional Basin Study	2010
8	Truckee River Basin Study	2010
9	Hood River Basin, Oregon Water Supply and Demand Study	2011
10	Klamath River Basin Study	2011
11	Lower Rio Grande Basin Study	2011
12	Sante Fe Basin Study	2011
13	Los Angeles Basin Stormwater Conservation Study	2012
14	Pecos River Basin Study	2012
15	Republican River Basin Study	2012
16	Sacramento-San Joaquin River Basin Study	2012
17	Upper Washita Basin Study	2012

Reclamation Basin Study boundaries

Basin name

Colorado
Columbia
Klamath
Missouri
Sacramento - San Joaquin
Truckee
Upper Rio Grande
—— Rivers

Sources: Bureau of Reclamation; Map Resources (map).

All three of Reclamation's completed Basin Studies projected climate change to result in warming and changes in precipitation that will alter the snow cover and runoff that supply water to the river basins, although the changes may be difficult to predict with certainty for any particular location and time. For example, the Colorado River Basin study projected that snow cover will decrease in the basin as more precipitation falls as rain, rather than snow, and warmer temperatures cause earlier melting. As a result, the runoff in the basin is generally projected to decrease—except in the northern Rockies. The study concluded that without additional

Appendix II: Locations and Initial Results of
the U.S. Army Corps of Engineer's Pilot
Studies and Bureau of Reclamation's Basin
Studies

water management actions, a wide range of future imbalances in supply and demand are plausible, primarily because of the uncertainty in future water supplies.

The completed Basin Studies also found that climate change is expected to contribute to long-term imbalances in water supply and demand. The completed Basin Studies also identified, with varying degrees of specificity, possible adaptation strategies to address the projected effects of climate change on water resources. For example, the Colorado River Basin Study identified various combinations of potential adaptation strategies to address projected water supply and demand imbalances. The study noted that the purpose of identifying these strategies was not to select a single, best strategy, but rather to recognize that there are various ways to address projected water imbalances in the basin, and that each approach has positive and negative implications that should be considered in future planning efforts. Agency officials and study participants told us that Reclamation has formed workgroups to further refine the strategies and identify options that should then be evaluated through feasibility studies. In contrast, the Yakima River Basin Study identified a more specific set of adaptation strategies for which feasibility studies are planned. Nonfederal stakeholders, including those representing agricultural and the environmental interests, told us they are collaboratively pursuing state funding to initiate the feasibility studies.

Reclamation policy officials and several other basin stakeholders—including state water managers, environmental advocates, and local water providers—told us that a key outcome of the completed Basins Studies is the establishment of a shared view of how climate change will impact the basins and their water management infrastructure. Reclamation policy officials, as well as basin stakeholders representing environmental and tribal interests, told us that the Basin Studies represent Reclamation's first concerted efforts at holistic planning in the river basins, taking into account not only the needs and concerns of irrigation users, but also the interests of tribes, recreational users, environmental advocates, and others. A state water manager told us that a prior river basin planning effort had largely been unsuccessful due to the lack of involvement or opposition by environmental and tribal interests, and several stakeholders commended Reclamation for working to ensure that the views of a wide range of stakeholders, including environmental and tribal interests, were considered in the Basin Studies.

Appendix III: GAO Contact and Staff Acknowledgments

GAO Contact	Steve D. Morris, (202) 512-3841 or morriss@gao.gov
Staff Acknowledgments	In addition to the individual named above, Elizabeth Erdmann, Assistant Director; Brad Dobbins; Richard Johnson; Mick Ray; Jeanette Soares; Lorelei St. James; and Sarah E. Veale made key contributions to this report. Nirmal Chaudhary, John Delicath, Cindy Gilbert, and Armetha Liles provided additional technical assistance.